WHEN SCIENTISTS SPLIT AN ATOM, CITIES PERISHED

WAR BOOK FOR KIDS
CHILDREN'S MILITARY BOOKS

In this book, we're going to talk about the consequences when scientists learned how to split the atom. So, let's get right to it!

World War II began in 1939. There were already many powerful weapons that were being used in warfare. However, the atomic bomb was just a theory and had not yet been designed. Through the work of Albert Einstein, scientists had realized that the energy contained within the atom was enormous.

Atomic Bomb Explosion

Devastating Atomic Bomb Explosion

If an atom could be split, a devastating explosion would be the result. Entire cities could be destroyed and hundreds of thousands of lives could be lost with just one bomb.

THE WORK OF ALBERT EINSTEIN

When the Nazis came into power in Germany, Einstein, who was Jewish, was in danger. Before the war, he came to the United States to live and work. By the time Einstein came to the US in the 1930s he was famous for his theories of relativity. He had completed a large body of work at that point including his well-known equation $E = mc^2$.

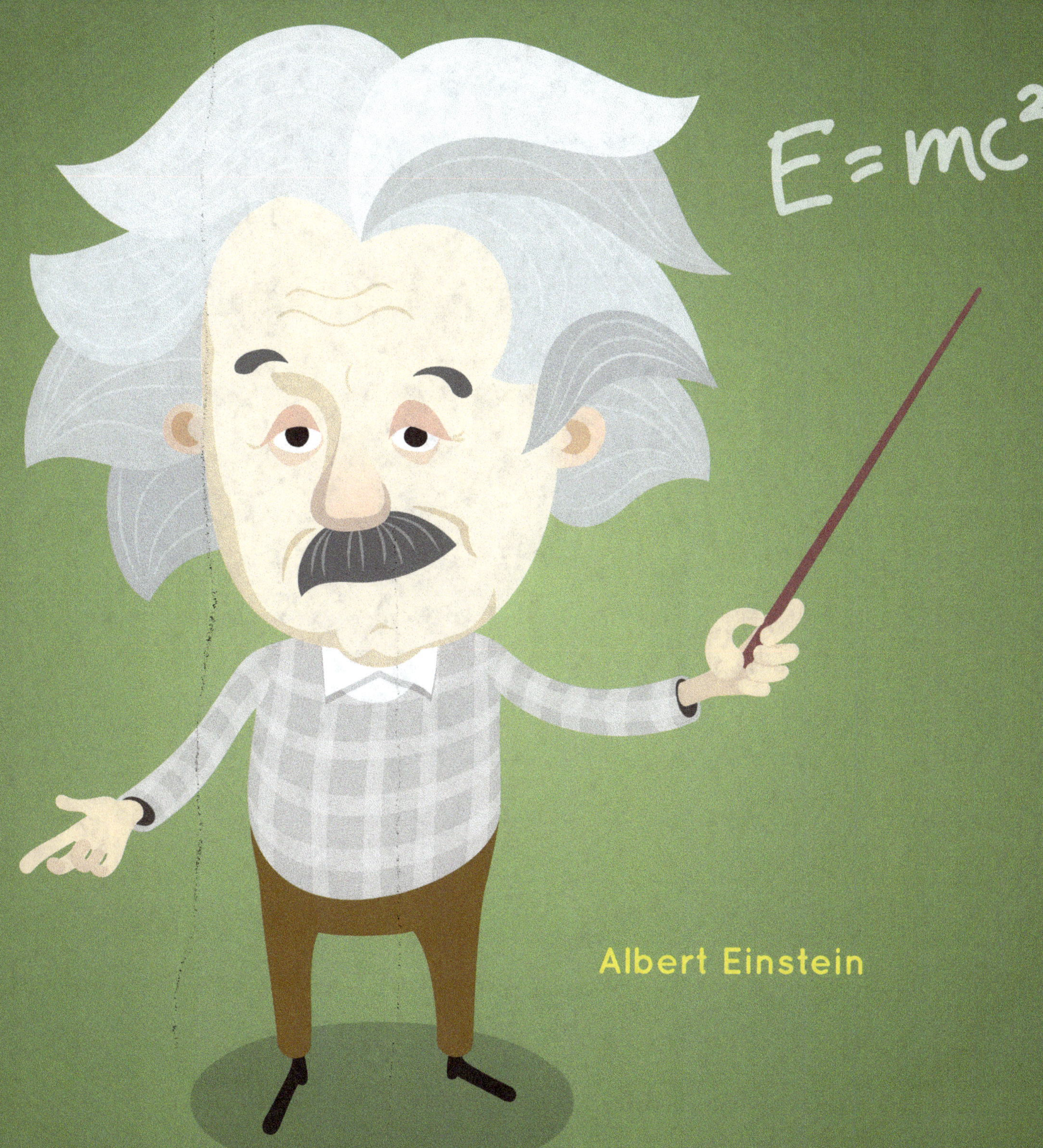

E=mc²
Albert Einstein

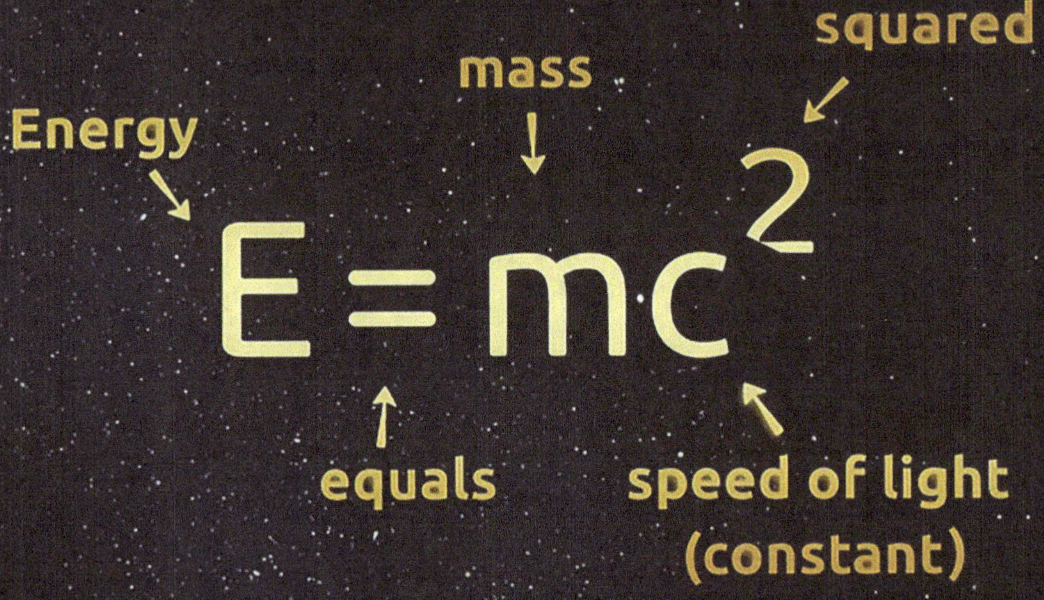

The variables in his formula are easy to understand but the theories behind it are complicated. The variable **E** stands for the amount of an object's energy. The **m** variable represents the object's mass.

The variable **c** stands for the speed of light, which is a constant and doesn't change. Einstein's equation told scientists that the energy locked up inside the atom was very powerful.

His equation was essential to the creation of nuclear energy as a new energy source. It could also be used for the basis of making bombs that were more dangerous than any mankind had ever created before.

Several physicists who had been working on nuclear experiments came to talk with Einstein about the development of bombs based on his theories. When Einstein saw how close this technology was to becoming a reality, he became very alarmed.

Along with a fellow physicist Leo Szilard he wrote a letter to then-president Franklin Delano Roosevelt informing him of his concerns if the United States wasn't the first to create the atomic bomb.

Adolf Hitler
He was worried that Hitler and the military in Germany would gain the power to use the atomic bomb first.

Manhattan Project Facility

THE MANHATTAN PROJECT

President Roosevelt didn't waste any time. He immediately began a program for the necessary research as well as the development of the atomic bomb. At the beginning, the program wasn't very big, but as the threat escalated, the United States government added funding and top scientists to the project, which was now named "The Manhattan Project."

It was clear that the atomic bomb could be a deciding factor in the war. Many of the participating scientists were originally from Germany and had escaped during the Nazi takeover. By the time the project was over, $2 billion dollars had been spent on the creation of a type of bomb that could potentially wipe out all mankind. Over 200,000 people were working on its research and development.

J. Robert Oppenheimer

The lead scientist was J. Robert Oppenheimer who was later called "the father of the A-bomb." After the bombs were dropped in Japan, Oppenheimer and many other scientists who had worked on the atomic bomb regretted their participation in creating the deadly weapon.

THE FIRST ATOMIC BOMB

Once the atomic bomb was ready, it had to be tested. On the 16th of July in 1945, the initial bomb was set off in the desert of New Mexico. The result was a huge explosion that was the same energy level as 18,000 tons of dynamite. Scientists estimated that the temperature at the core of the explosion was three times the heat at the sun's center.

Atomic bomb testing

The success of this test led to mixed feelings. Although the scientists working on the project felt that they had met their goal, they were concerned because of the destruction they knew the bomb would cause.

They knew that it was powerful enough to cause mass destruction of cities and populations. When President **Harry S. Truman** heard of the successful test he remarked that the United States now had possession of the most horrific bomb in the world's history.

Harry S. Truman

Bomb explosion

THE DECISION TO DROP THE BOMB

President Truman was faced with a very difficult decision. Germany had lost the war and in Europe the war was over. However, Germany's ally, Japan, would not admit defeat. In order to end the war, America might have had to invade Japan to force them to surrender.

Truman's advisors told him that half a million to a million American as well as Allied soldiers would perish in such an invasion. Faced with these two evils, Truman decided to drop atomic bombs on Japan to force their surrender.

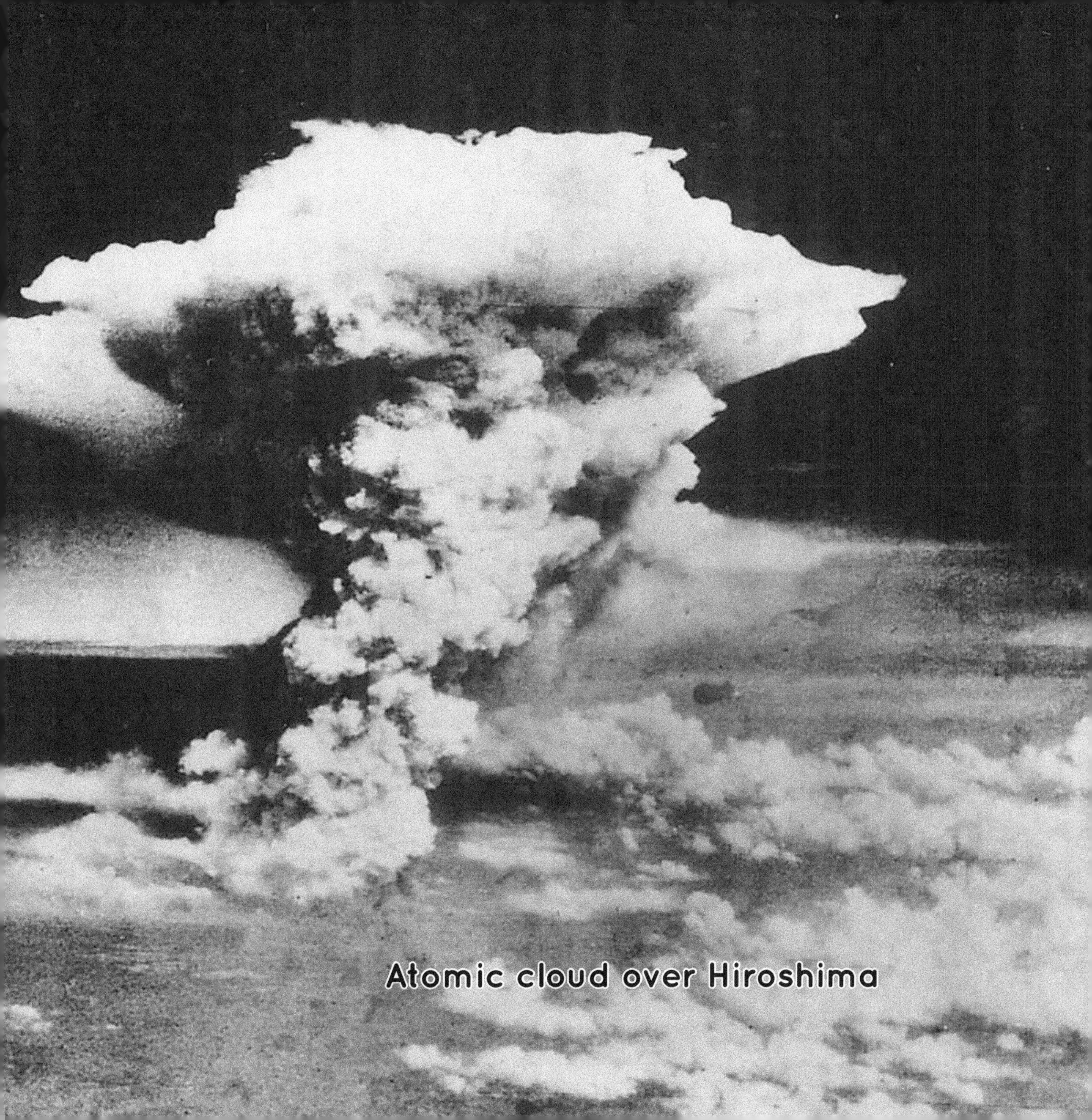
Atomic cloud over Hiroshima

Bomb dropped at Hiroshima

THE ATOMIC BOMB IS DROPPED ON HIROSHIMA

Tokyo, the Japanese capital, was already largely destroyed due to the war. The city of Hiroshima was selected as the first target. It hadn't been destroyed during the war so the effects of the atomic bomb would seem even more devastating.

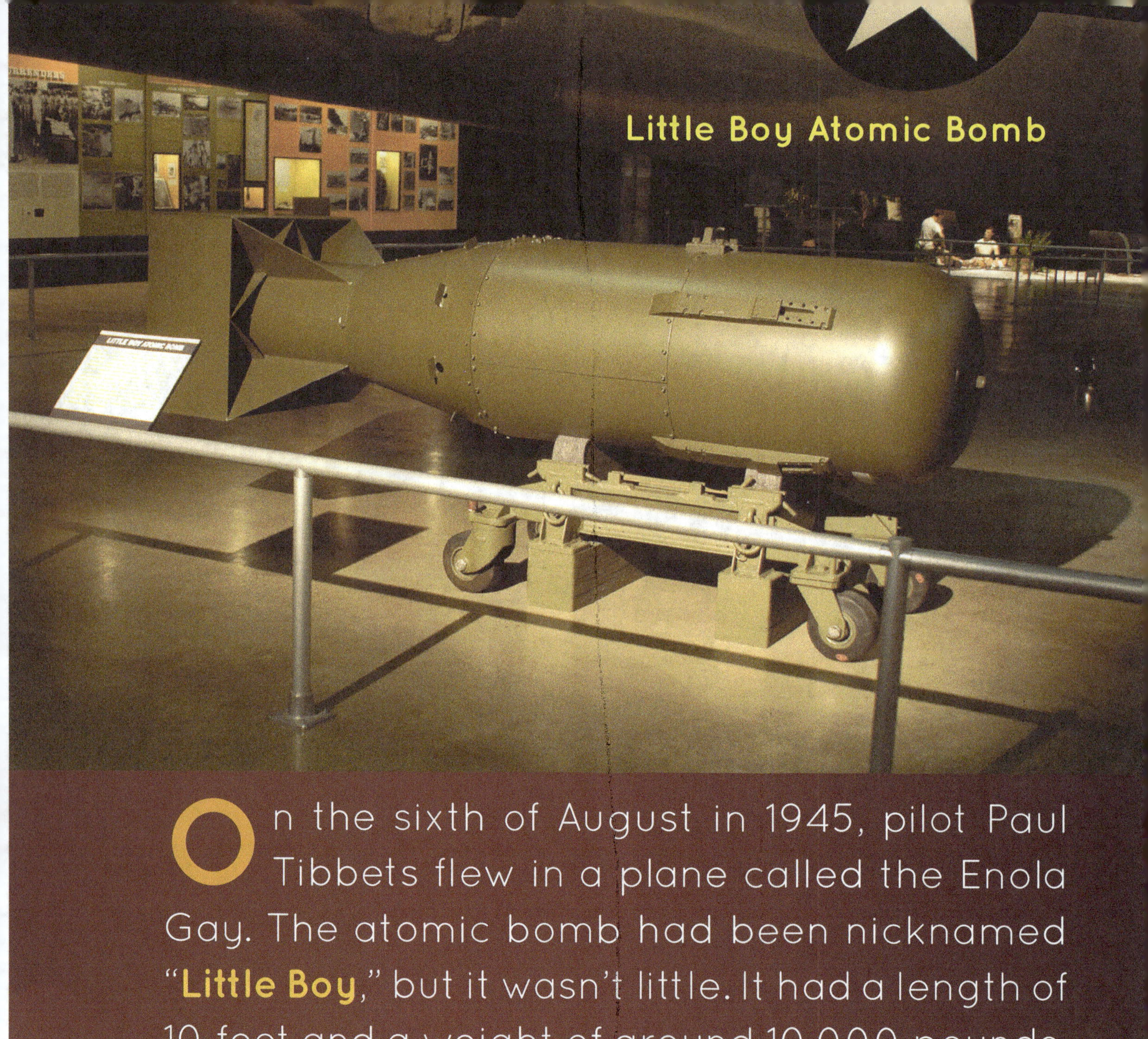

On the sixth of August in 1945, pilot Paul Tibbets flew in a plane called the Enola Gay. The atomic bomb had been nicknamed "**Little Boy**," but it wasn't little. It had a length of 10 feet and a weight of around 10,000 pounds.

Paul Tibbets

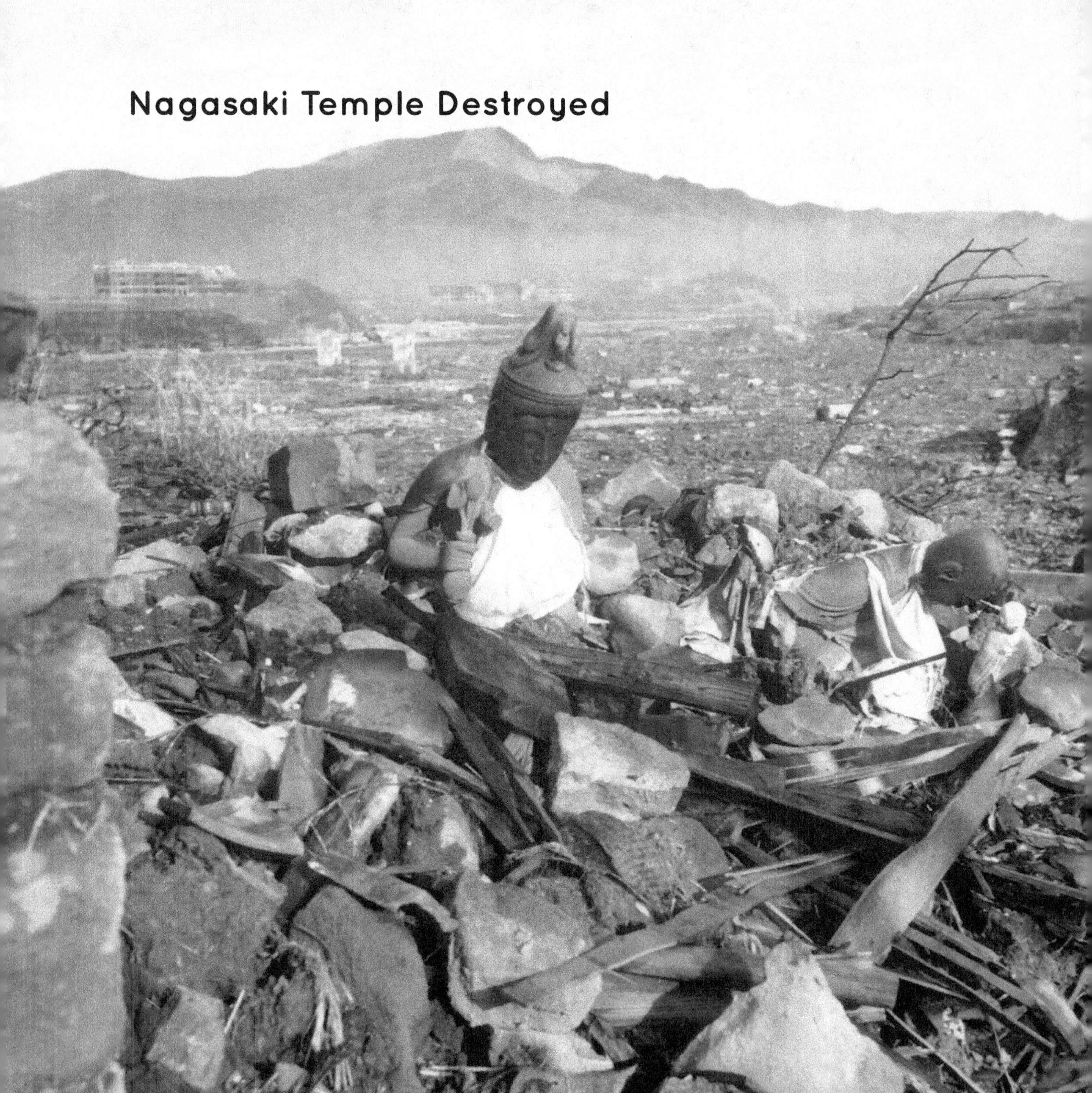
Nagasaki Temple Destroyed

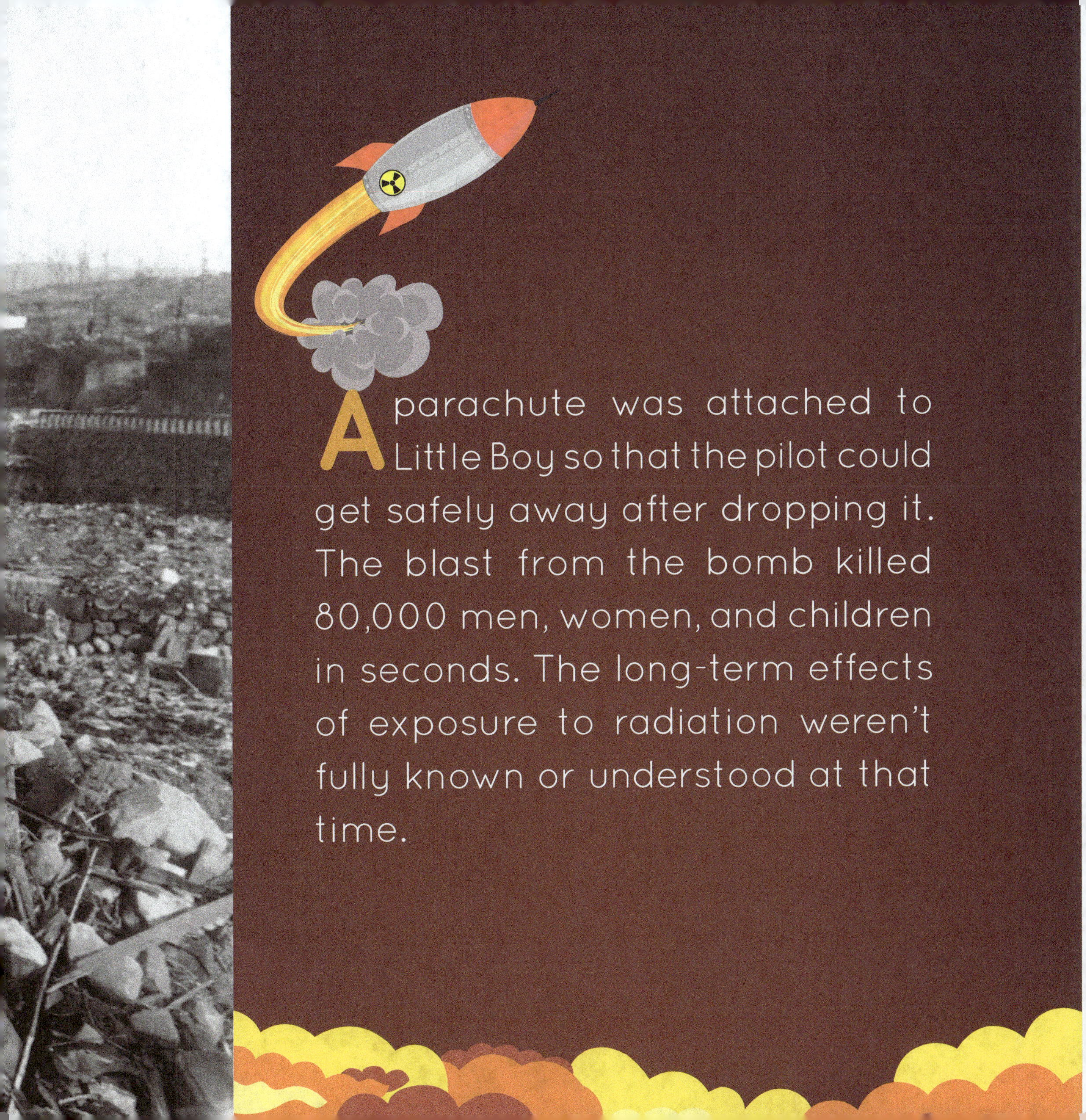

A parachute was attached to Little Boy so that the pilot could get safely away after dropping it. The blast from the bomb killed 80,000 men, women, and children in seconds. The long-term effects of exposure to radiation weren't fully known or understood at that time.

In the following months, about the same number of people died from radiation burns and radiation sickness in conjunction with other illnesses and starvation. Although one of the reasons that Hiroshima had been selected was because it had a large military force, most of the people who died were civilians.

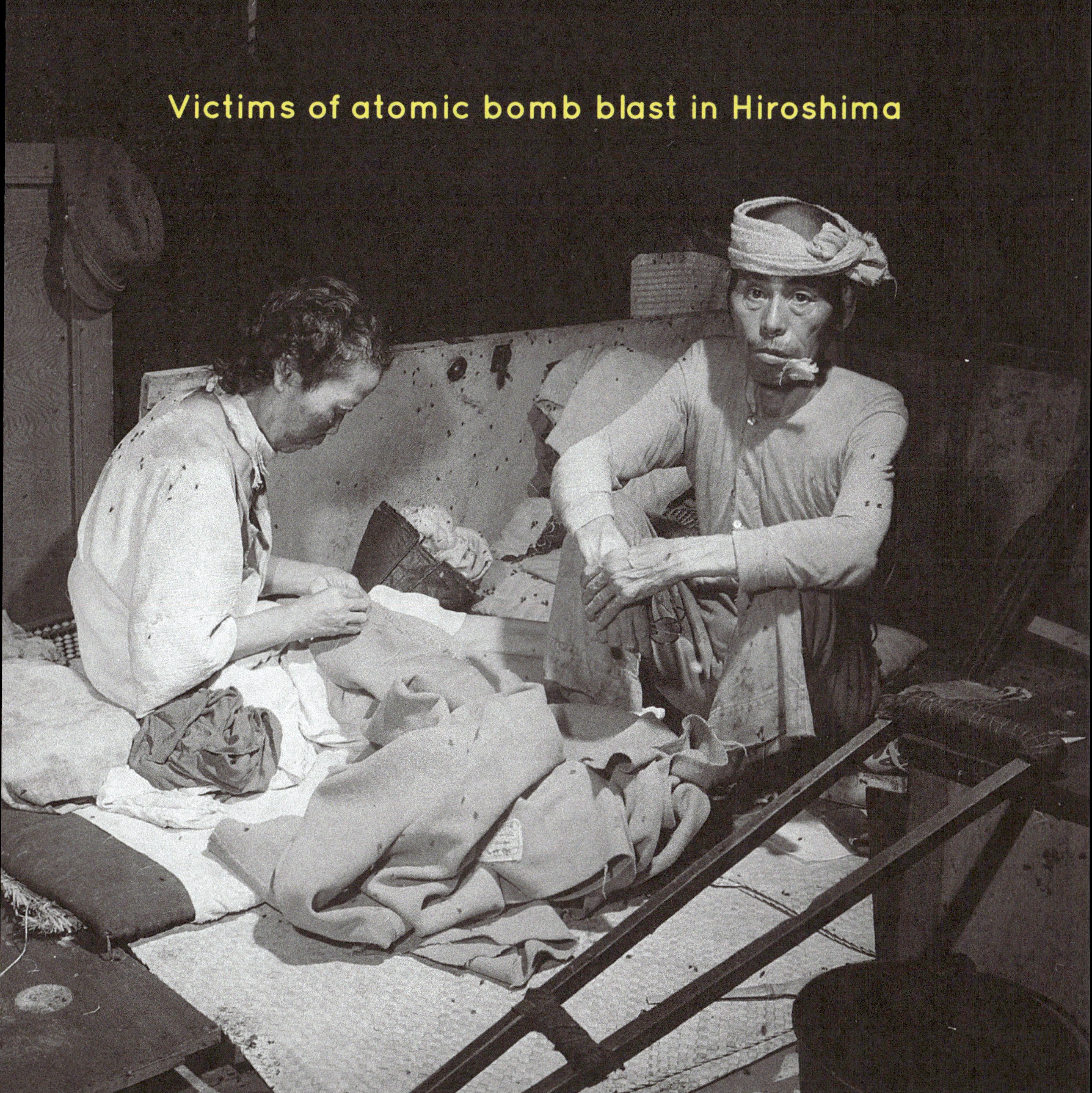
Victims of atomic bomb blast in Hiroshima

Emperor Hirohito

THE ATOMIC BOMB IS DROPPED ON NAGASAKI

Even though Emperor Hirohito of Japan was aware of the destruction Japan was facing, he didn't surrender. On the ninth of August, the United States dropped another A-bomb on the city of Nagasaki. This atomic bomb was called "Fat Man" and was even more powerful since it was made from plutonium, instead of uranium like Little Boy.

The devastation was widespread with about 40,000 people killed instantly and another 40,000 killed in the subsequent months from aftereffects of the radiation.

Little Boy and **Fat Man** were the only two atomic bombs ever used in warfare. The United States had a series of bombs planned if the Japanese didn't surrender.

Japan surrendered to the United States

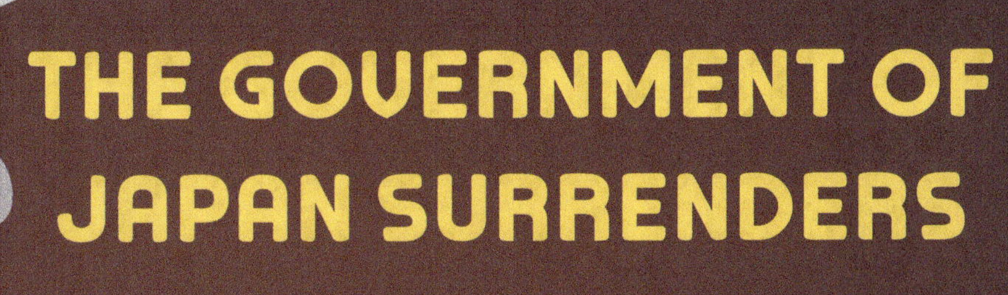

THE GOVERNMENT OF JAPAN SURRENDERS

On August 15, the Emperor of Japan surrendered to the United States. He talked to his people on the radio. It was the very first time the Japanese people had heard Hirohito's voice.

DID THE UNITED STATES WARN THE JAPANESE PEOPLE?

A fter the Potsdam Conference in Germany when the United States and its allies negotiated the conditions of Germany's surrender, the allies issued a separate declaration.

The declaration stated that if Japan didn't unconditionally surrender that they would face "utter destruction."

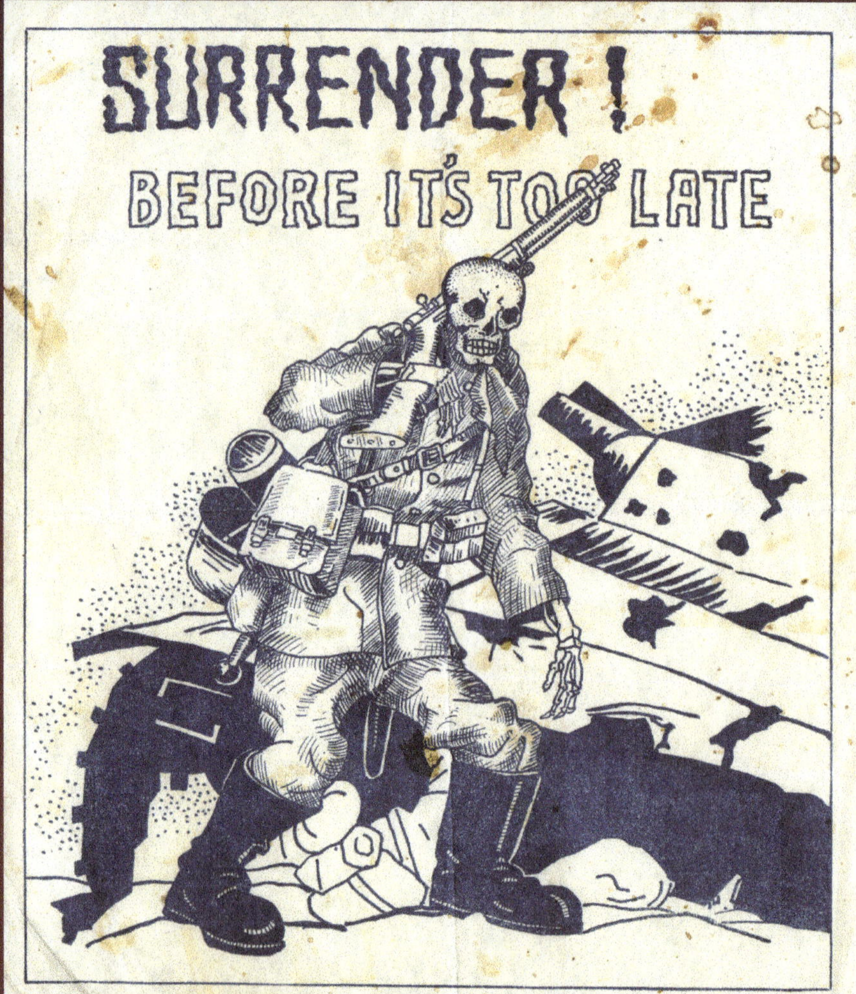

U.S. Propaganda leaflet dropped in Japan urging civilians to evacuate cities before U.S. bombing. Ca. 1944. World War 2.

The United States also dropped leaflets on Japanese soil that gave warnings of the impending disaster. There's some debate as to whether these leaflets were truly warnings or simply being used as psychological warfare designed to get the Japanese to surrender.

HIBAKUSHA

Hibakusha means "people that were affected by the explosion." The long-term consequences for these people have been devastating. The Japanese government records the names of those who have died from radiation-related illnesses. The numbers are over 300,000 for Hiroshima and over 170,000 for Nagasaki. In addition to the physical pain that was caused, the Hibakusha and their children have suffered discrimination in Japan. The public believed that their diseases could be passed from generation to generation although that hasn't been scientifically proven.

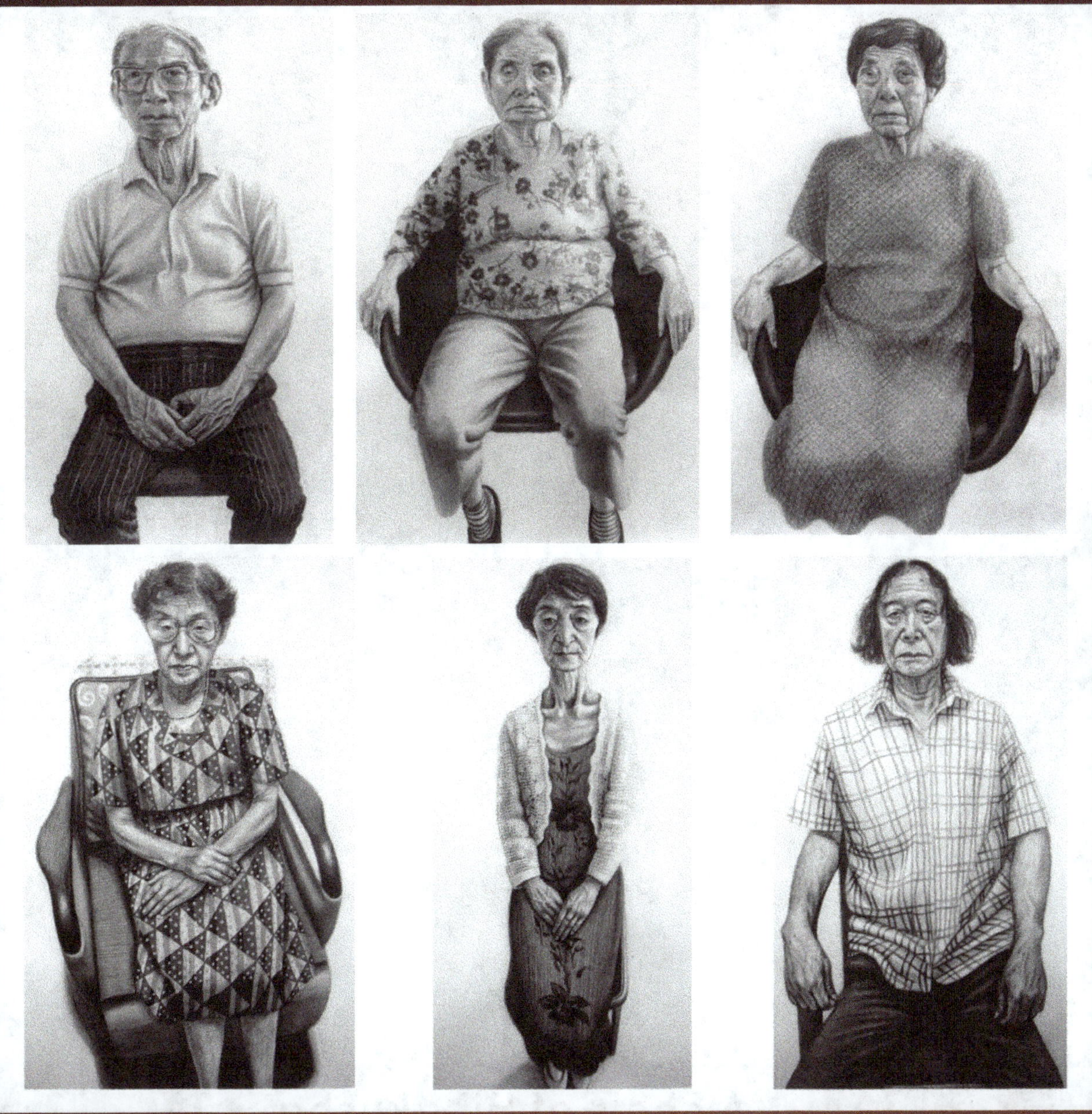

Hibakusha

A choir of Hibakusha
(atomic bomb survivors)

As a result, they were denied jobs and sometimes were not seen as suitable marriage partners. Today these survivors and their children are fighting for nuclear weapons to be banished worldwide.

SUMMARY

Einstein's work on relativity had given scientists information about the immense power of splitting the atom. After talking with other physicists, Einstein realized that there was technology being created to use the splitting of the atom to make powerful atomic bombs. He and a fellow physicist wrote to President Franklin Delano Roosevelt to warn him of the dangers of the Germans getting their hands on such bombs. The President established "The Manhattan Project" to research and develop A-bombs.

President Franklin Delano Roosevelt

A survivor of the atomic bombing of Nagasaki, tells young people about his experience.

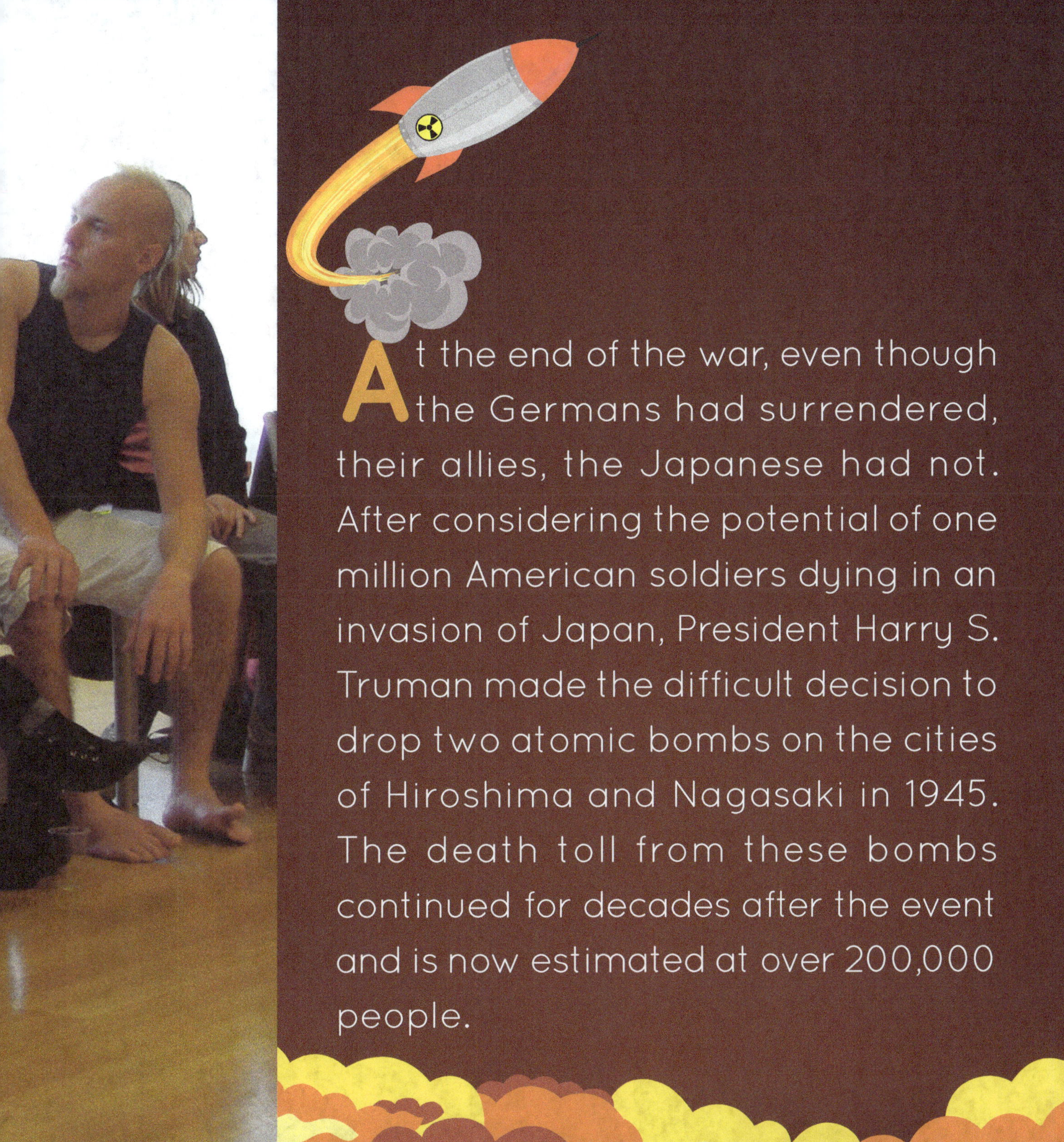

At the end of the war, even though the Germans had surrendered, their allies, the Japanese had not. After considering the potential of one million American soldiers dying in an invasion of Japan, President Harry S. Truman made the difficult decision to drop two atomic bombs on the cities of Hiroshima and Nagasaki in 1945. The death toll from these bombs continued for decades after the event and is now estimated at over 200,000 people.

Now that you know more about the atomic bomb you may want to find out more information about the science of atomic particles in the Baby Professor book *Elementary Particles: The Building Blocks of the Universe*.

Visit

BABY PROFESSOR
EDUCATION KIDS

www.BabyProfessorBooks.com

to download Free Baby Professor eBooks
and view our catalog of new and exciting
Children's Books